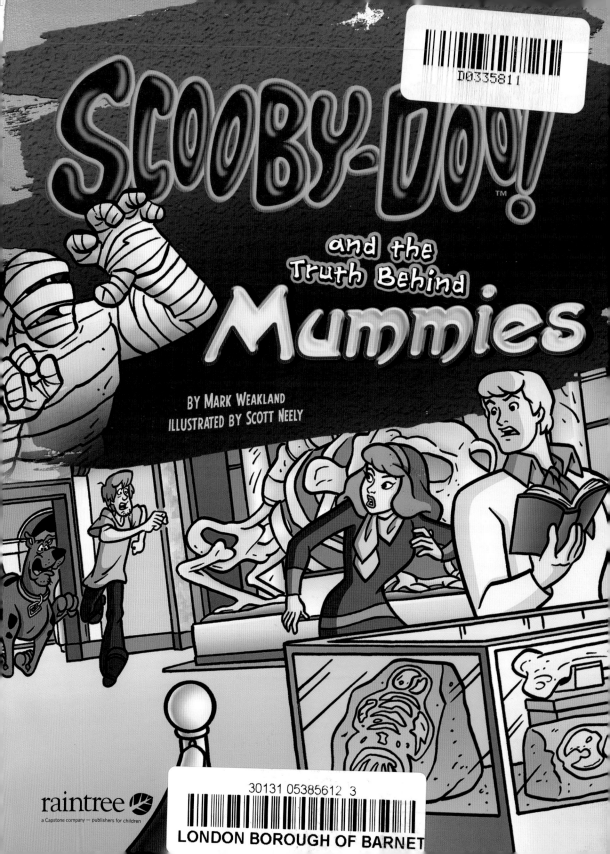

SCOOBY-DOO!

and the
Truth Behind

Mummies

BY MARK WEAKLAND
ILLUSTRATED BY SCOTT NEELY

raintree
a Capstone company — publishers for children

Raintree is an imprint of Capstone Global Library Limited, a company incorporated in England and
Wales having its registered office at 7 Pilgrim Street, London, EC4V 6LB — Registered company
number: 6695582

www.raintree.co.uk
myorders@raintree.co.uk

CAPG34578

Text © Capstone Global Library Limited 2015
The moral rights of the proprietor have been asserted.

Editorial Credits:
Editor: Shelly Lyons
Designer: Ted Williams
Art Director: Nathan Gassman
Production Specialist: Tori Abraham

ISBN 978-1-4062-8897-1 (paperback)
18 17 16 15 14
10 9 8 7 6 5 4 3 2 1

British Library Cataloguing in Publication Data
A full catalogue record for this book is available from
the British Library.

Acknowledgements
We would like to thank the following for permission to reproduce
photographs: Design Elements: Shutterstock: ailin1, AllAnd,
hugolacasse, Studiojumpee

The illustrations in this book were created traditionally, with
digital colouring.

We would like to thank Elizabeth Tucker Gould, Professor of English,
Binghamton University for her invaluable help in the preparation of
this book.

Every effort has been made to contact copyright holders of
material reproduced in this book. Any omissions will be rectified
in subsequent printings if notice is given to the publisher.

All the internet addresses (URLs) given in this book were valid at
the time of going to press. However, due to the dynamic nature
of the internet, some addresses may have changed, or sites may
have changed or ceased to exist since publication. While the
author and publisher regret any inconvenience this may cause
readers, no responsibility for any such changes can be accepted
by either the author or the publisher.

Printed and bound in China.

Scooby-Doo and the gang were visiting the museum. They were excited about seeing the new exhibits. But Scooby and Shaggy had gone missing.

"This museum is so big," said Velma. "I hope they haven't got lost."

The silence was broken when Shaggy and Scooby burst into the room. "Rummy!" barked Scooby.

"He thinks he saw a mummy!" yelped Shaggy. "In the Ancient Egyptian room!"

Oh, they're dead. But legendary mummies, like those in films, come back from the dead.

That's true! Even though they're not alive, they shuffle, moan and chase people.

RUH-ROH!

In ancient Egypt the body of a dead King or Queen was washed, prepared and wrapped in strips of cloth bandages. But a mummy of legend only becomes a living monster if someone curses it. Or if it can't stand to be without the person it loves!

"A human body," said Fred. "Ancient Egyptians removed the internal organs. They left the heart in place. Then the body was dried with a salt called natron and wrapped in linen."

"Why?" asked Scooby.

"To prepare it for the afterlife," said Velma.

"The brains were removed too," added Daphne. "But in stories and films, mummies are clever, even without brains."

"Then the body was put in a coffin. Sometimes the coffin was then put into a bigger stone coffin called a sarcophagus," said Velma. "Then the sarcophagus was put into a tomb."

Mummies from films and stories want to rest in peace. They like their cosy, quiet tombs. But treasure hunters and scientists disturb their sleep. This irritates mummies.

Ri'd be grouchy.

Where do real mummies come from?
Mummies come from countries such as Egypt, Chile, Peru and China. Ice mummies have been found in the mountains of Italy and Peru.

Mummies in films usually stumble out of ancient Egyptian pyramids.

Or any very dry place – even a high mountain cave.

"How do we know if a mummy is chasing us?" asked Shaggy nervously.

"In films mummies often moan," said Fred. "And shuffle their feet."

"Roaning and ruffling?" Scooby said.
"And a mummy is wrapped in cloth,"
said Velma. "That's a dead giveaway!"

PIZZA

"Yes," said Fred. "In films and stories, mummies are very strong. They carry a curse that affects those who disturb them. Sometimes they have special powers too."

"Some can move objects just by thinking. That's called telekinesis," said Velma.

"And some control insects, wind or sand with their minds," added Daphne.

"Bugs!" yelled Shaggy.

"Yuck!" barked Scooby.

In some ways mummies and zombies are the same. In stories and films, both rise from their graves and are undead creatures.

But a mummy's flesh is dry, not rotten like a zombie's.

And zombies want to eat people's brains. Mummies aren't interested in doing that.

"You don't have to worry," said Daphne. "Legendary
mummies are strong, but they move slowly.

"Another way to protect yourself is with fire," said Fred.
"Mummies catch fire easily because of their bandages.
If you set one on fire, it will be destroyed."

"Rokay!" said Scooby.

GLOSSARY

ancient from a long time ago

internal organs parts of the inside of the body; the heart, lungs, liver and kidneys are organs

legend story handed down from the past

linen cloth made from a flax plant

telekinesis power to move things with the mind

tomb room or building that holds a dead body

BOOKS

Egyptian Myths and Legends (All About Myths), Fiona Macdonald (Raintree, 2013)

Uncovering Mummies: An Isabel Soto Archaeology Adventure (Graphic Expeditions), Agnieszka Biskup (Raintree, 2010)

Zombies Vs Mummies: Clash of the Living Dead (Monster Wars), Michael O'Hearn (Raintree, 2012)

WEBSITES

www.bbc.co.uk/history/ancient/egyptians
Uncover the rich history of ancient Egyptians and read interesting stories about mummies from around the world.

www.britishmuseum.org
Browse this website to discover amazing facts about mummies and learn about the mummification process.

INDEX